how to market trivia night

Skyrocket Your Bar's Popularity with Successful
Trivia Marketing - Actionable Strategies for
Attracting Crowds and Boosting Sales

Trivia Night for Bars and Restaurants
Book Two

jon nelsen

life level up books, llc

How to Market Trivia Night: Skyrocket Your Bar's Popularity with Successful Trivia Marketing - Actionable Strategies for Attracting Crowds and Boosting Sales

Copyright © 2023 by Jon Nelsen

Disclaimer Notice:

Please note the information contained within this document is for educational and entertainment purposes only. All effort has been executed to present accurate, up to date, reliable, complete information. No warranties of any kind are declared or implied. Readers acknowledge that the author is not engaged in the rendering of legal, financial, medical or professional advice. The content within this book has been derived from various sources. Please consult a licensed professional before attempting any techniques outlined in this book.

By reading this document, the reader agrees that under no circumstances is the author responsible for any losses, direct or indirect, that are incurred as a result of the use of the information contained within this document, including, but not limited to, errors, omissions, or inaccuracies.

This book is written for entertainment purposes only. The statements made in this book do not necessarily reflect the present market at the time of reading or current views of the author. Furthermore, the author accepts no responsibility for actions taken by the reader as a result of information presented in this book.

contents

introduction

. . .

HELLO, I'm Jon Nelsen, an experienced trivia host with years of hosting successful trivia nights in breweries, bars, and restaurants. My journey has allowed me to witness first-hand the transformative power of trivia nights – they're not just fun games, but pivotal events that significantly boost customer retention, attract new patrons, and drive up profits. I've seen bars turn from quiet corners to vibrant community hubs on trivia nights, and I'm here to share these insights with you.

In a world where every bar competes for the spotlight, one event stands out as a beacon of collective joy and spirited rivalry: trivia night. It's more than just a game; it's an experience, a gathering, a vibrant community event that turns a regular evening into a memorable one. "How to Market Trivia Night: Skyrocket Your Bar's Popularity with Successful Trivia Marketing" is your guide to transforming these evenings into a magnet for fun-seekers and trivia aficionados alike.

Imagine a bar buzzing with excitement, filled with

groups of friends huddled over their tables, whispering and laughing as they ponder over the next question. This isn't just any night; this is your trivia night, a night where your establishment becomes the heart of the community. But how do you get there? How do you turn your trivia night from an idea into an event that people eagerly anticipate week after week?

Marketing is the secret sauce. But not just any marketing – a kind that understands the pulse of your local community, speaks directly to the hearts of your customers, and wraps it all in an irresistible package of fun and challenge. This book is about learning that art. It's about understanding your audience, using the tools at your disposal, and constantly adapting to the ever-changing tastes of your patrons.

We'll explore the power of social media, not as a mere platform for promotion, but as a space to build a community, to connect with your audience, and to share the vibrant personality of your bar. It's about turning posts into conversations, followers into fans, and social media buzz into a crowded bar.

But let's not forget the charm of personal touch. Email marketing, often overlooked, is a powerful tool in your arsenal. It's about crafting messages that resonate, about speaking directly to your customers, reminding them of the fun that awaits at your trivia night.

Partnerships, word-of-mouth, traditional marketing, online presence – each is a thread in the tapestry of your marketing strategy. We'll weave these threads together, creating a cohesive, comprehensive approach that touches every aspect of your marketing efforts.

And then, there's adaptation – the ability to listen to feedback, to learn from your successes and setbacks, and to keep improving. Your trivia night is a living, breathing entity that evolves with your audience. It's about staying ahead of the curve, anticipating changes, and being ready to pivot when necessary.

This book isn't just a collection of strategies; it's a conversation. It's about sharing experiences, insights, and practical tips that you can implement right away. It's about inspiring you to take your trivia night from a mere event to a highlight of the local social calendar.

So, let's embark on this journey together. Let's explore, learn, and grow. Let's turn your trivia night into the event everyone talks about, the event that draws crowds and keeps them coming back for more. Here's to your success, to the laughter and cheers that await, and to the nights when your bar is the brightest star in the neighborhood. Welcome to "How to Market Trivia Night." Let's make some magic happen.

harnessing social media to amplify your trivia night

. . .

Turn Your Followers into Fanatics – Engaging
Your Online Community

SOCIAL MEDIA ISN'T JUST about collecting followers like vintage stamps; it's about turning them into die-hard fans of your bar's trivia night. Think of it as not just attracting a crowd, but creating a cult following (minus the weird rituals). You're not just a bar owner; you're a community leader in the digital age.

Let's face it, social media is the town square of the 21st century, and your bar is the hip new spot everyone needs to check out. But how do you transform passive scrollers into enthusiastic participants at your trivia night? The secret sauce is engagement, and I don't mean putting a ring on it.

First things first, understand your audience. Are they trivia nerds who revel in obscure historical facts or pop culture buffs who can quote every line from "Friends"? Once you've got that down, it's time to speak their language. Your posts should be as flavorful as your bar's signature cocktail, offering a mix of entertainment, information, and, most importantly, a reason to leave their couches.

Think about it, why should someone swap their comfy pajamas for real pants and join your trivia night? Your content needs to scream, "This is the place to be!" Showcase the fun, the laughter, and maybe even the occasional facepalm moment from your trivia nights. Remember, FOMO (fear of missing out) is a powerful motivator.

Now, let's talk about interaction. This isn't a monologue; it's a conversation. When followers comment, dive into that dialogue like it's the last slice of pizza. It's about building relationships, not just broadcasting messages. Ask questions, run polls, maybe even throw in a trivia question or two. Get them thinking, "Hey, I knew that! I should go show off my smarts."

And here's where the magic happens – user-generated content. Encourage your patrons to post their trivia night shenanigans. There's nothing more convincing than seeing real people having a real good time. It's like having a bunch of mini-marketers at your disposal. Plus, it's free!

But don't just take my word for it. According to Sprout Social, 90% of consumers will purchase from a brand they follow on social media. That's a lot of potential trivia buffs walking through your door.

Of course, it's not all rainbows and butterflies. Negative comments? Handle them with grace and a touch of humor. A well-managed complaint can turn a critic into a fan. Remember, the internet remembers everything – except for your passwords, apparently.

Sprinkle in some exclusive social media offers. "Show this post and get a bonus point at trivia night" – sounds tempting, right? It's about adding value to their experience, making them feel like part of an exclusive club. Who doesn't love feeling special?

But let's not forget, this isn't just about packing the room; it's about creating an experience. An experience so good, they'll want to share it, tweet it, and bring their friends next time. And before you know it, your bar is not just a bar; it's a community hub.

So, let's recap – know your audience, create engaging content, foster interactions, leverage user-generated content, and add value through exclusives. Simple, right? Well, not quite, but definitely doable.

Remember, at the end of the day, it's not just about likes and shares. It's about creating a connection, a bond, that no algorithm can replicate. Your bar's trivia night isn't just an event; it's a gathering of minds, a celebration of community. And your role? You're not just a host; you're the maestro of an unforgettable social symphony.

As you embark on this journey of turning followers into fanatics, keep this in mind: social media is your stage, and every post is a performance. Make it count.

Local Legends Unleashed: Mastering Social Media to Build Your Brand and Community

In the digital age, social media for local businesses is like a Swiss Army knife – versatile, indispensable, and surprisingly powerful. Gone are the days when local marketing meant just a signboard and word of mouth. Today, with a few taps on a screen, a local bar can become the talk of the town, and social media is the stage where this transformation happens.

Understanding the impact of social media on local businesses is akin to recognizing the power of a well-placed billboard in Times Square. It's not just about visibility; it's about creating a space where your brand's personality shines, engaging with the community in real-time. For instance, a local coffee shop that shares its daily specials or behind-the-scenes glimpses on Instagram isn't just selling coffee; it's selling an experience, a slice of local life that resonates with customers.

But before diving into the social media pool, it's crucial to know who's swimming in it. Identifying your target audience on various platforms is the cornerstone of any successful marketing strategy. Are your potential patrons millennials scrolling through Instagram, or are they busy professionals networking on LinkedIn? Maybe they're Gen Zers, crafting their aesthetic on TikTok. Knowing where your audience hangs out is like knowing where to cast your fishing line – it's half the battle won.

Once you've identified your audience, it's time to talk about the role of social media in building a community around your brand. This is where the magic happens. It's one thing to post content; it's another to create a space where customers feel like they're part of a tribe. A local brewery, for example, can use Facebook Groups to create a beer enthusiasts' club, where members share their favorite brews and stories. This isn't just marketing; it's community building. It's about striking a chord with your audience, making them feel like they're not just buying a product or service, but becoming part of a story.

Consider the local bakery that posts pictures of their mouth-watering pastries on Instagram. Each post is not just a photo; it's an invitation to indulge in a sensory experience. Or the bookstore that tweets book recommendations – it's not just selling books; it's fostering a community of readers.

However, this doesn't mean you bombard your followers with sales pitches. The art of social media marketing lies in balancing promotional content with content that educates, entertains, and engages. It's about creating a narrative that your audience wants to follow. Think of it as a TV show; if all you do is show commercials, viewers will change the channel.

In conclusion, social media's power in local marketing cannot be understated. It's a dynamic, interactive, and incredibly effective way to reach out to your community, understand their needs, and engage with them on a level that traditional marketing can't match. It's about being authentic, responsive, and most importantly, human. After all, at the heart of every local business is a story waiting to be told, and social media is the perfect narrator. So go ahead, tell your story, build your community, and watch as your local business becomes a local legend.

Viral Verve: Unlocking the Secrets to Magnetic Social Media Content for Trivia Nights

Creating content that sticks in your audience's mind like that catchy tune from a TV commercial is an art, especially in the realm of social media for trivia nights. It's not just about posting; it's about posting content so engaging that your followers can't help but hit 'share'. Let's dive into the alchemy of crafting content that turns your trivia night from just another event into the talk of the digital town.

Designing Engaging and Shareable Trivia-Related Posts

The key to engaging posts is to make them as addictive as the final season of your favorite series. You want your followers to anticipate your posts like they do the next episode. Here's how:

- **Tell a Story**: People love narratives. Share anecdotes about past trivia nights, the epic fail or surprising win, and watch your engagement soar.
- **Visuals are King**: Use bright, eye-catching images or short videos. Think of visuals as the pizza toppings that make your content irresistible.
- **Interactive Content**: Polls, quizzes, and questions aren't just engaging; they're like a digital handshake with your audience.

Leveraging Hashtags and Trends for Broader Reach

Navigating the world of hashtags and trends can be like trying to find your way through a corn maze, blindfolded. However, when done right, they can be your golden ticket to viral content.

- **Relevant Hashtags**: Use hashtags like a GPS for your content. They guide users to your posts. But remember, overloading on hashtags can look as desperate as double texting.
- **Trending Topics**: Jump on the bandwagon of trending topics. If there's a trending meme, twist it to fit your trivia theme. It's like being the cool kid in school everyone wants to hang out with.

Timing Your Content for Maximum Engagement

Timing in social media is like timing in comedy – get it wrong, and you've lost your audience. Posting when your audience is most active is crucial. According to Sprout Social, the best times to post can vary based on industry and audience habits. But don't just rely on statistics; test and learn. Monitor when your posts get the most interaction, and adjust your schedule accordingly. It's like tuning your guitar before a big performance.

In this digital age, where attention spans are shorter than a goldfish's memory, making your posts count is crucial. It's not just about bombarding your followers with content; it's about delivering quality content that speaks to them, engages them, and makes them want to be a part of your trivia community.

Remember, the goal is to create content so engaging that missing your trivia night feels like missing a New Year's Eve party. Your content should not just echo in the digital hallways of social media; it should resonate with the personality of your brand and the interests of your audience.

As we navigate the intricate dance of social media marketing, let's not lose sight of its essence – connection. It's about connecting with your audience on a level that goes beyond likes and shares. It's about creating a space where they feel seen, heard, and part of something bigger. Your trivia night isn't just an event; it's a community, and your content is the bridge that brings people together.

In the end, remember that crafting irresistible social media content is a mix of art and science. It's about understanding your audience, being authentic, and sometimes, just going with your gut. After all, in the fast-paced world of social media, sometimes the best strategy is to be unapologetically you.

Cultivating a Digital Family: The Art of Fostering an Engaged Online Community

Building an online community is like hosting a never-ending house party. You're not just inviting people over; you're making them feel like they belong, like they're part of something special. For bar owners and trivia enthusiasts, this is your arena to turn casual followers into a loyal tribe.

Encouraging Interaction and Feedback

First, let's talk about sparking conversations. Social

media is your microphone, and every post is an opportunity to start a dialogue. But how do you get people talking?

- **Ask Questions**: This isn't rocket science; it's social science. Post questions that provoke thought or nostalgia. "What was your favorite trivia win?" Watch as memories and comments flood in.
- **Respond to Comments**: This is where the magic of connection happens. Each response is a thread in the fabric of your community. Be authentic, be witty, and most importantly, be present.
- **Regular Updates**: Keep your followers in the loop. Share what's new, be it a trivia theme or a new brew. It's like giving them a VIP pass to your bar's backstage.

Creating a Sense of Belonging Among Followers

Everyone wants to belong, to feel like they're part of a club. Here's where you turn your followers into family.

- **Exclusive Groups**: Create a Facebook or WhatsApp group for your trivia regulars. It's like having a private room in a bustling party.
- **User-Generated Content**: Encourage your followers to share their trivia night experiences. It's not just content; it's a scrapbook of shared memories.
- **Recognition and Rewards**: Who doesn't love a shoutout? Feature your regulars on your social media. Make them the stars of your show.

Organizing Online Trivia Events as a Teaser

Now, let's get to the exciting part - online trivia events. These are teasers, appetizers before the main course at your bar.

- **Regular Online Trivia Nights**: Host a mini-trivia session online. It's a taste of the fun, a lure for the bigger event at your bar.
- **Interactive Platforms**: Use platforms like Zoom or Instagram Live. The key is interactivity; you want your audience playing, not just watching.
- **Special Themes**: Create themes for your online trivia. From '90s pop culture to sci-fi, themes are the spice that keeps the game zesty.

Remember, the goal is not just to build a following but to cultivate a community. It's about making each follower feel seen, heard, and valued. It's about creating a space where people come for the trivia but stay for the camaraderie. Your online community is where these stories unfold and where the magic happens. It's where a follower becomes a friend, a customer becomes a regular, and a regular becomes family.

Building an online community is an ongoing journey, a dance of engagement, belonging, and connection. It's about striking that delicate balance between leading the conversation and listening to the chorus of voices in your community. It's about being more than a bar or a trivia host; it's about being a gathering place, a hub of laughter, debate, and shared experiences.

As you embark on this journey, remember that every

post, every interaction, and every event is a brick in the foundation of your community. So build it with care, with love, and with the joy that comes from bringing people together. After all, in this digital age, the heart of a community beats not just in the physical space of your bar, but in the vibrant, lively, and ever-growing world of social media.

creating buzz with email marketing

. . .

Captivate Your Audience – Crafting Emails They Can't Ignore

Mastering the Inbox: The Secret to Creating Unforgettable Emails

IN THE VAST ocean of digital communication, crafting an email that not only survives the ruthless currents of the inbox but also shines like a beacon, is an art. Gone are the days of bland, generic emails that are as forgettable as last week's lunch special. In today's fast-paced digital world, your email needs to be more than just words on a screen; it needs to be an experience.

Think about it. Every day, your audience is bombarded with a barrage of emails, all vying for attention. What makes yours stand out? Is it the witty subject line that makes them chuckle? The personalized touch that makes them feel seen? Or the compelling content that leaves them wanting more? The answer is all of the above and more.

Crafting Unforgettable Content

Creating an email that captivates your audience starts with understanding them. Dive into their world. What are their likes, dislikes, hopes, and fears? This isn't just about selling a product or service; it's about connecting on a human level. Here's where the magic happens:

- **Storytelling**: Weave a narrative. People may forget facts, but they never forget a good story. Make your email a short, gripping tale that they're eager to follow.
- **Personalization**: Address your readers by name, reference their interests, make them feel special. It's like receiving a letter from a friend rather than a corporation.

- **Value**: Offer something more than just a sales pitch. Share tips, insights, a piece of knowledge. Make opening your email a rewarding experience.

The Power of the Subject Line

Your subject line is your first, and often only, chance to grab attention. Make it count. A great subject line is like a movie trailer - intriguing, exciting, and promising an adventure. Be bold, be funny, be mysterious. Just don't be boring.

Timing is Everything

Sending an email is like planting a seed; timing is crucial. Research the best times to send emails when your audience is most likely to engage. It's not just about avoiding the spam folder; it's about landing in their inbox when they're most receptive.

Encouraging Interaction

What's an email if not a conversation starter? End with a question, a call to action, an invitation to engage. Make them feel like they're part of a dialogue, not just a monologue.

In this digital age, where emails are as common as stars in the sky, being just another star won't do. You need to be a comet, leaving a trail of light that's impossible to ignore.

As you embark on this journey of email mastery, remember, it's not just about what you say; it's about how you say it. It's about crafting an experience that resonates, connects, and ultimately, converts. Your email is more than a message; it's a key to a door. A door that leads to deeper engagement, lasting relationships, and yes, increased sales.

Mastering the art of email communication is a journey. It's a process of trial and error, of understanding and adapting. But the reward is worth the effort. Because when you do it right, you're not just sending an email; you're starting a conversation, building a relationship, and creating an unforgettable experience. So go ahead, make your mark in the inbox, and watch as your emails become the highlight of your audience's day.

The Power of Personalization: Mastering the Art of Email List Building

In the digital marketing universe, an email list is like a gold mine waiting to be tapped. It's not just a list of addresses; it's a gateway to a community of individuals who are interested in what you have to offer. Building and segmenting your email list is the first step in turning a casual browser into a loyal customer.

Building Your Email List: More than Just Collecting Addresses

Building an email list is akin to building a relationship. It's not about how many people you can get to sign up; it's about finding those who genuinely want to engage with your brand.

- **Offer Value**: People won't just give away their email addresses without a good reason. Offer something valuable - a discount, a freebie, or insightful content.

- **Optimize Your Sign-Up Process**: Make it easy and tempting. A pop-up on your website, a sign-up button on your social media pages, or a quick form at the end of your blog posts can work wonders.
- **Be Transparent**: Let people know what they're signing up for. Is it a newsletter, weekly deals, or exclusive content? Clarity builds trust.

Segmentation: The Art of Personalized Communication

Once you have your list, it's time to segment it. Segmentation is about understanding that not all subscribers are the same. Tailoring your communication to different groups within your list can significantly increase engagement.

- **Demographics**: Age, location, and gender can determine how you personalize your emails.
- **Behavior**: Track how subscribers interact with your emails. Who opens them regularly? Who clicks on the links? Use this data to tailor your content.
- **Interests**: Send relevant content based on their interests. If someone signed up from a page about vegan recipes, they probably won't be interested in your latest barbecue sauce.

Understanding the Value of Direct Communication

Email is a direct line to your audience. It's personal, it's one-on-one. Unlike social media, where your content can get lost in the noise, an email lands straight in their inbox. This direct communication is powerful and should be used wisely.

- **Build Relationships**: Use emails to build a connection. Share stories, behind-the-scenes glimpses, and personal insights.
- **Feedback and Interaction**: Encourage replies. Ask for feedback. Make your subscribers feel heard and valued.

Compliance and Best Practices in Email Marketing

Now, let's talk compliance. With great power comes great responsibility. Adhering to email marketing laws and best practices is crucial.

- **Permission-Based Marketing**: Always get consent before adding someone to your list. No one likes unsolicited emails.
- **The CAN-SPAM Act**: Familiarize yourself with the CAN-SPAM Act. It sets the rules for commercial email, establishes requirements for commercial messages, and gives recipients the right to have you stop emailing them.
- **GDPR Compliance**: If you have subscribers from the European Union, you need to be GDPR compliant. This means respecting user privacy and data protection rights.

Remember, an email list is more than just a marketing tool; it's a community of individuals who have chosen to listen to what you have to say. Treat them with respect, provide value, and they will become more than just subscribers; they'll become advocates for your brand.

Building and managing an email list is a journey of understanding and respecting your audience. It's about communication, personalization, and compliance. It's an opportunity to speak directly to individuals who are interested in your story, your brand, and what you have to offer. So, embrace the power of email marketing, and watch as it transforms not just your business, but also the way you connect with your audience.

Crafting Emails That Speak: A Guide to Captivating Your Audience

In the world of email marketing, where the average person receives 121 emails per day, crafting content that stands out is like finding a needle in a digital haystack. The key lies in creating emails that are not just read, but remembered. Let's break down the art of designing emails that captivate your audience, from gripping subject lines to a perfect blend of information and promotion, topped with effective visuals and calls-to-action.

Designing Attention-Grabbing Subject Lines

Your subject line is your first impression, and in the world of email, it's often the only one you get. It's the make-or-break moment where your email decides its fate - to be opened or lost in the abyss of the inbox.

- **Be Intriguing, Not Misleading**: Craft subject lines that pique curiosity but stay true to the content. Think of it as the headline of your favorite newspaper article.

- **Personalize**: Add a personal touch. Using the recipient's name or referencing their recent activity can boost open rates.
- **Keep it Short and Sweet**: With most emails opened on mobile, brevity is key. Aim for less than 50 characters to ensure your entire subject line is visible on mobile screens.

Balancing Informative and Promotional Content

Striking a balance between informative and promotional content in your emails is like walking a tightrope. Lean too far either way, and you risk losing your audience.

- **Educate, Then Sell**: Offer your readers valuable information or insights before pitching your product or service. It builds trust and adds value to your email.
- **Storytelling**: Everyone loves a good story. Use narratives to illustrate your points and then subtly tie in your product or service.
- **Segmentation is Key**: Tailor your balance of content based on the segment of your audience. What works for new subscribers may not resonate with long-term customers.

Utilizing Visual Elements and Calls-to-Action Effectively

Visuals can turn an average email into a visual feast,

while a well-placed call-to-action (CTA) is the nudge your readers need to take the next step.

- **A Picture is Worth a Thousand Words**: Use high-quality images or graphics to break the text and keep the reader engaged. Ensure they complement, not clutter, your message.
- **CTAs that Convert**: Your CTA should be clear, compelling, and easy to find. Whether it's a button or a hyperlink, make sure it stands out.
- **Mobile Optimization**: With over 60% of emails opened on mobile devices, ensure your visuals and CTAs are mobile-friendly.

In crafting your email content, remember that you're not just competing against other businesses; you're vying for attention against everything in your reader's inbox. Your email should not just aim to inform or sell; it should aim to connect. It should speak directly to your reader's interests, needs, and desires.

The art of email content strategy lies in creating a blend of captivating subject lines, a balanced mix of informative and promotional content, and the strategic use of visual elements and CTAs. It's about understanding the human on the other side of the screen and crafting an email experience that speaks to them. Remember, in the crowded world of the inbox, your email is not just a message; it's a story, a conversation, a connection waiting to happen. So go ahead, write emails that don't just communicate but captivate.

Email Timing and Testing: Unlocking the Secrets to Skyrocketing Engagement

In the digital age, sending an email is akin to casting a line into the vast sea of the internet, hoping for a bite. The trick to catching the big fish – maximizing open rates and engagement – lies in not just what you send but when and how you send it. This segment delves into the strategic nuances of email timing, the science of A/B testing, and the art of analyzing campaign performance to transform your email marketing into a magnet for audience attention.

Optimal Email Timing: It's All in the Timing

Picture this: you craft the perfect email, hit send, and... crickets. Timing is crucial. Sending an email at the right time can mean the difference between being seen or being lost in the abyss of an overcrowded inbox.

- **Understand Your Audience**: Are they early birds or night owls? Knowing when your audience checks their email increases the chances of your email being opened.
- **Industry Standards and Trends**: While there's no one-size-fits-all answer, studies suggest midweek, midday sends tend to perform well. But remember, your audience is unique.
- **Time Zone Tango**: If your audience is global, consider time zones. It's like hosting a worldwide party – you want everyone to arrive at the right time.

A/B Testing: The Laboratory of Email Marketing

A/B testing in email marketing is like conducting a science experiment. You change one variable, keep everything else constant, and observe the results. This methodical approach can significantly optimize your email content.

- **Test One Element at a Time**: Whether it's the subject line, the call to action, or the email design, change one element per test to accurately measure its impact.
- **Use a Significant Sample Size**: Ensure your test groups are large enough to provide reliable data. Small sample sizes can give misleading results.
- **Analyze and Adapt**: Use the insights from A/B testing to continually refine your emails. It's an ongoing process of learning and improving.

Analyzing Campaign Performance: Beyond Opens and Clicks

Evaluating the success of an email campaign goes beyond just tracking open and click-through rates. It's about understanding the story behind the numbers.

- **Engagement Metrics**: Look at metrics like click-to-open rates and time spent reading the email. These metrics give deeper insights into how engaging your content is.
- **Feedback Loops**: Encourage and monitor feedback from your subscribers. Their comments and suggestions are invaluable for tailoring content to their interests.
- **Holistic View**: Consider how your email campaigns fit into your broader marketing

strategy. Are they driving the desired actions,
like website visits or purchases?

Remember, the goal of your email campaign is not just
to be seen but to resonate with your audience. It's about
creating content that speaks to them, arriving in their inbox
at just the right moment, and continually evolving based on
feedback and data.

In the world of email marketing, there's no magic
formula for success. It's a dance of timing, testing, and
analysis – a dance that requires patience, persistence, and a
willingness to adapt.

Maximizing open rates and engagement in email
marketing is a multifaceted endeavor. It requires a deep
understanding of your audience, a commitment to testing
and learning, and a keen eye for analyzing data. By
mastering these elements, you can turn your email
campaigns into a powerful tool for connecting with your
audience, building relationships, and driving conversions.
So, set sail into the vast ocean of email marketing, armed
with these strategies, and watch as your engagement rates
soar.

leveraging local partnerships and sponsorships

. . .

Unite and Conquer – Forging Alliances for Mutual Success

Strategic Alliances: Mastering the Art of Finding Ideal Partners and Sponsors

NAVIGATING the world of business partnerships and sponsorships is like embarking on a treasure hunt. It's an adventure filled with opportunities, challenges, and the potential for great rewards. Understanding how to identify the right partners and sponsors is a crucial skill for any entrepreneur or business owner looking to expand their reach and amplify their impact. This chapter is dedicated to unraveling the secrets of forming strategic alliances that go beyond mere transactions to become mutually beneficial relationships.

Unlocking the Benefits of Local Partnerships

Local partnerships are like the secret sauce to your business recipe. They add a unique flavor that can enhance your brand's appeal. But why go local?

- **Community Connection**: Local partnerships help you tap into the heart of your community, building a network of support and recognition.
- **Shared Resources**: Collaborating with local businesses can lead to shared resources, reducing costs and increasing efficiency.
- **Increased Visibility**: Joining forces with other local entities can amplify your marketing efforts, making your business more visible to potential customers.

Choosing Compatible Businesses and Organizations

Selecting the right partners and sponsors is not about picking names out of a hat. It's a strategic decision that requires careful consideration.

- **Alignment of Values**: Look for businesses and organizations that share your core values and business ethics. This alignment is key to a harmonious and productive partnership.
- **Complementary Strengths**: Identify potential partners who bring something different to the table - a skill, resource, or market access that complements your own offerings.
- **Long-Term Potential**: Consider the long-term potential of the partnership. It's not just about what they can do for you today, but how you can grow together in the future.

Crafting Win-Win Proposals for Potential Partners

Once you've identified potential partners, the next step is to approach them with a proposal that's hard to refuse.

- **Tailor Your Approach**: Customize your proposal to address the specific needs and interests of the potential partner. Show them that you've done your homework.
- **Highlight Mutual Benefits**: Clearly articulate how the partnership will benefit both parties. It's about creating a win-win situation where everyone gains.
- **Be Transparent and Realistic**: Set realistic expectations and be transparent about what you

can offer. Honesty and clarity lay the
groundwork for trust and a lasting partnership.

In this journey of finding the right partners and sponsors, remember that it's not just about what you gain, but
also about what you contribute. Successful partnerships are
built on a foundation of mutual respect, shared goals, and a
commitment to each other's success.

As business strategist and author Simon Sinek says, "If
you want to go fast, go alone. If you want to go far, go
together." This mantra holds true in the realm of partnerships. By joining forces with the right partners, you not only
expand your capabilities but also embark on a journey
towards sustainable growth and success.

In conclusion, identifying potential partners and sponsors is an art that requires insight, strategy, and a keen eye
for opportunities. It's about understanding the unique landscape of your business, recognizing the potential in others,
and crafting proposals that bring mutual benefits. As you
turn the pages of this chapter, you will be equipped with
the knowledge and tools to navigate this exciting aspect of
business growth, laying the groundwork for partnerships
that transform and elevate your business.

Fostering Lasting Partnerships: The Roadmap to Relationship Success

In the bustling world of business, building and
nurturing relationships with partners is akin to cultivating a
garden. It requires patience, effort, and a touch of creativity. This segment delves into the nuances of maintaining
consistent communication, collaborating on events and
promotions, and measuring and sharing success, essential

components in ensuring that your business relationships blossom and thrive.

Maintaining Consistent Communication: The Lifeline of Business Relationships

Just as a plant needs water to grow, consistent communication is vital to nurturing your business relationships. It's about creating a dialogue that goes beyond transactional interactions.

- **Regular Updates**: Share regular updates on your projects and business developments. It keeps partners in the loop and demonstrates your commitment to transparency.
- **Feedback Channels**: Establish open channels for feedback. Encourage honest and constructive discussions to foster trust and understanding.
- **Personal Touch**: Don't let your communications become robotic. Personalize your interactions. Remembering a birthday or congratulating a partner on a personal achievement can go a long way.

Collaborating on Events and Promotions: Synergy in Action

Collaborating on events and promotions is like a dance – it requires coordination, rhythm, and a shared vision.

- **Joint Ventures**: Plan events or promotions that leverage each partner's strengths. It could be co-hosting a webinar, a joint sale, or a community event.

- **Shared Goals**: Ensure that your collaborative efforts have shared goals. It's not just about pooling resources; it's about achieving something greater together.
- **Cross-Promotion**: Utilize each other's marketing channels for cross-promotion. This approach broadens your reach and provides value to your partner.

Measuring and Sharing Success: Celebrating Milestones Together

Measuring and sharing successes with your partners is crucial. It's about recognizing achievements and learning from challenges.

- **Define Success Metrics**: Agree on what success looks like. Is it increased sales, brand exposure, or customer engagement? Clear metrics pave the way for objective assessment.
- **Regular Reviews**: Schedule regular meetings to review the progress of your partnership. Discuss what's working and what isn't, and adjust your strategies accordingly.
- **Celebrate Milestones**: Acknowledge and celebrate milestones. Whether it's the success of a joint campaign or the anniversary of your partnership, recognition fosters a sense of shared accomplishment.

In the journey of building and nurturing business relationships, remember that every partner is unique. Understanding their goals, challenges, and working styles is key to creating a harmonious and productive relationship.

As Steve Jobs once said, "Great things in business are never done by one person. They're done by a team of people." This sentiment rings especially true in the realm of business partnerships. By effectively communicating, collaborating on mutually beneficial initiatives, and celebrating successes together, you're not just building a network; you're building a community of support and opportunity.

The art of fostering lasting partnerships lies in the details - the regular check-ins, the collaborative projects, the shared victories, and even the shared setbacks. It's about building a foundation of trust, respect, and mutual benefit that stands the test of time. As you embark on this path, equip yourself with these strategies, and watch as your business relationships transform into pillars of strength and growth for your enterprise.

Synergizing Success: Elevating Partnerships to New Heights

In the dynamic landscape of modern business, partnerships are not just about handshakes and contract signings. They are about creating synergies that propel both parties to new heights of success. This involves co-hosting events, leveraging each other's networks, and crafting innovative co-branded merchandise and offers. Let's dive into how these strategies can maximize the impact of partnerships, turning them into a powerhouse of mutual growth and success.

Co-Hosting Events and Cross-Promotions: The Power of Collaboration

Co-hosting events and engaging in cross-promotions are like hosting a grand feast where both partners bring their best dishes to the table. It's a celebration of collaboration that offers a plethora of benefits.

- **Expanded Reach**: By pooling resources and audiences, events can attract a wider, more diverse crowd, offering greater exposure for both partners.
- **Shared Costs and Resources**: Collaborating reduces the burden of costs and resources, making it economically efficient while maintaining the quality and scale of the event.
- **Enhanced Brand Perception**: Joint events can elevate the brand image of both partners, showcasing them as dynamic, cooperative, and customer-focused.

Leveraging Each Other's Networks: The Art of Networking

Leveraging each other's networks in a partnership is like tapping into a goldmine of opportunities. It's about using the strength of combined networks to unlock doors that might otherwise remain closed.

- **Referrals and Introductions**: Utilize each other's contacts for introductions to potential clients, suppliers, or even employees, expanding your business reach.

- **Shared Expertise**: Exchange knowledge and expertise. This can lead to innovative solutions and new strategies, beneficial to both businesses.
- **Joint Marketing Efforts**: Collaborate on marketing campaigns, combining your marketing prowess to create impactful strategies that resonate with a broader audience.

Creating Branded Merchandise and Collaborative Offers: A Tangible Connection

The creation of co-branded merchandise and collaborative offers is a tangible manifestation of partnership. It's a strategy that not only promotes the brands but also symbolizes the unity of the partnership.

- **Exclusive Products or Services**: Develop unique products or services that combine the strengths of both partners. This exclusivity can attract both customer bases and even new ones.
- **Branding Opportunities**: Co-branded merchandise serves as a powerful marketing tool, enhancing brand visibility and recognition.
- **Strengthen Customer Loyalty**: Exclusive offers or products can foster a sense of belonging and loyalty among customers, enhancing customer retention for both partners.

In this world of collaborations, remember that partnerships are like a dance. It requires rhythm, understanding, and a shared vision to create a performance that captivates the audience - in this case, the market.

As Henry Ford once said, "Coming together is a beginning, staying together is progress, and working together is success." This sentiment perfectly encapsulates the essence of maximizing partnership impact. It's about coming together with a shared goal, nurturing the relationship through consistent effort, and collectively working towards achieving success.

Maximizing the impact of partnerships is about harnessing the collective strengths of each partner to create something greater than the sum of its parts. It's a strategic ballet of co-hosting events, leveraging networks, and creating co-branded ventures - all orchestrated with the goal of mutual growth and success. As you embark on this journey of partnership enhancement, let these strategies be your guide, helping you navigate the path to building fruitful, lasting collaborations that stand the test of time and change.

mastering word-of-mouth marketing

· · ·

The Art of the Buzz – Transforming Patrons into Promoters

Harnessing the Whispered Power: The Transformative Role of Personal Recommendations in Business

IN A WORLD BOMBARDED with digital advertising, the quiet power of a personal recommendation remains an unrivaled force in the business landscape. This unassuming yet potent tool, especially in the realm of trivia night experiences, can turn a casual visitor into a loyal advocate. This chapter explores the profound impact of word-of-mouth endorsements, the art of creating an unforgettable trivia experience, and the strategies to encourage customers to become vocal supporters of your business.

Understanding the Impact of Word-of-Mouth

Word-of-mouth is the old-school social network that has been influencing decisions long before the advent of digital media. It's the trusty friend whose advice we seek and trust implicitly.

- **Trust Factor**: Recommendations from friends or family carry a weight of trust that paid advertisements can rarely match. They come with a personal stamp of approval.
- **Extended Reach**: One person's positive experience can ripple out to a vast network, multiplying the reach far beyond the original conversation.
- **Authenticity**: Personal recommendations come with a genuineness that resonates with potential customers. They speak the language of real experience, not marketing jargon.

Creating an Unforgettable Trivia Experience

An extraordinary trivia night is like a well-crafted story – it stays with the audience long after it's over. It's about crafting moments that are worth talking about.

- **Engagement is Key**: Make your trivia nights interactive and engaging. It's not just about the questions; it's about the experience.
- **Unique Themes and Formats**: Stand out by introducing creative themes or unique formats. This makes your event memorable and different from the usual trivia nights.
- **Foster a Community Feel**: Create an environment where people don't just come to play trivia, but to be part of a community. A sense of belonging can turn participants into passionate advocates.

Encouraging Customers to Share Their Experiences

Turning customers into storytellers of your brand is an art. It's about giving them stories worth sharing and making it easy for them to spread the word.

- **Incentivize Sharing**: Implement a referral program or incentives for customers who bring friends. Small gestures of appreciation can encourage sharing.
- **Social Media Savvy**: Make it easy for customers to share their experiences on social media. Create shareable moments,

hashtags, or photo ops during your trivia nights.

- **Gather Feedback and Act on It**: Show that you value customer opinions by actively seeking feedback and making improvements. This can turn even a neutral experience into a positive story.

In harnessing the power of personal recommendations, remember, it's not just about the immediate impact. It's about building a network of organic support that grows and strengthens over time.

Personal recommendations are the hidden gems in the marketing world. They might not be as flashy as a viral social media campaign, but their value and impact are undeniable. They build a foundation of trust and authenticity that can elevate a business from a simple venue to a community favorite.

Leveraging the power of personal recommendations is about more than just good service or an enjoyable trivia night. It's about creating experiences that resonate, that people want to talk about, and that align with the values and desires of your community. It's a journey of understanding your customers, connecting with them on a deeper level, and providing them with stories they are eager to share. Embrace this subtle yet powerful tool, and watch as it transforms your business, one whispered recommendation at a time.

Turning Customers into Champions: The Art of Incentivizing Referrals and Reviews

In today's fast-paced digital world, word-of-mouth has

evolved. It's no longer just about friends sharing recommendations over coffee; it's about customers turning into your brand's champions online. This segment of our chapter focuses on the strategies for incentivizing referrals and reviews, a vital element in modern-day marketing that can significantly amplify your brand's reach and reputation.

Implementing a Referral Program: A Win-Win Strategy

Implementing a referral program is like setting up a mutual appreciation society where both your customers and your business reap the rewards.

- **Simple and Appealing**: Keep your referral program easy to understand and participate in. Offer incentives that excite your customers – discounts, freebies, or exclusive access.
- **Communicate Clearly**: Promote your referral program through all your channels – email, social media, and in-person. Ensure your customers know how it works and what's in it for them.
- **Track and Optimize**: Use referral tracking software to monitor the program's performance. Adapt and tweak the program based on customer feedback and participation rates.

Encouraging Online Reviews and Feedback: Harnessing the Power of Customer Voice

Online reviews are the digital age's word-of-mouth.

They are testimonials of your service's quality and your brand's reliability.

- **Make It Easy**: Provide easy access for customers to leave reviews – direct links in emails, on receipts, or through your website.
- **Respond to Reviews**: Show that you value customer feedback by responding to reviews, both positive and negative. It demonstrates your commitment to customer satisfaction.
- **Incentivize Reviews**: Consider offering a small incentive for leaving a review. It could be a discount on their next purchase or entry into a contest. Remember, the goal is to encourage genuine feedback.

Rewarding Loyal Customers: Building a Community of Brand Advocates

Your loyal customers are your treasure trove, and rewarding them is not just good business; it's building a community.

- **Loyalty Programs**: Implement a loyalty program that rewards repeat business. Points systems, special discounts, and birthday offers are excellent ways to show appreciation.
- **Exclusive Experiences**: Offer your loyal customers something unique – a first look at a new product, an invite to a special event, or access to premium services.
- **Personalized Communication**: Recognize your regulars with personalized communication.

Acknowledge their support in newsletters or on social media, making them feel like a valued part of your business family.

Incentivizing referrals and reviews is about creating a cycle of positive experiences and appreciation. It's a strategy that not only enhances your brand's reputation but also strengthens the bond with your customers.

Remember, in the realm of business, your customers are your storytellers. They are the narrators of your brand's story in the vast digital landscape. By implementing effective referral programs, encouraging online reviews, and rewarding loyalty, you transform your customers into enthusiastic brand ambassadors.

The journey of incentivizing referrals and reviews is about understanding and leveraging the power of customer satisfaction. It's about turning happy customers into vocal advocates for your brand. As you explore these strategies, remember that the key is authenticity and appreciation. Genuine efforts to acknowledge and reward your customers' loyalty can turn them into powerful allies in your brand's growth story. Engage in this practice not just as a marketing strategy, but as a commitment to building lasting relationships with those who matter most to your business – your customers.

Empowering Your Brand with User-Generated Content: A Goldmine of Authenticity

In today's digital era, where content is king, there's a treasure trove often overlooked: user-generated content (UGC). This segment delves into how businesses can capitalize on the goldmine of photos, stories, and experiences shared by patrons, transforming them into powerful marketing tools. From hosting contests to showcasing customer experiences on various platforms, UGC is not just content; it's a testament to your brand's impact and authenticity.

Capitalizing on Photos and Stories Shared by Patrons

Every photo or story shared by a customer is a badge of honor, a sign of their engagement and endorsement. Here's how to make the most of this valuable content:

- **Create Shareable Moments**: Design your space or services with shareability in mind. Whether it's an Instagrammable spot in your store or a unique aspect of your service, create moments that customers want to capture and share.
- **Encourage Sharing**: Use signage, social media, and verbal cues to encourage patrons to share their experiences. Make sure they know your social media handles and hashtags.
- **Feature User Content**: Regularly feature user content on your platforms. It not only provides you with authentic material but also makes your customers feel valued and part of your brand story.

Hosting Contests and User-Generated Challenges

Contests and challenges are a brilliant way to engage

customers and generate a wealth of UGC. They add a fun, competitive element that encourages participation.

- **Design Engaging Contests**: Whether it's a photo contest, a hashtag challenge, or a story-sharing campaign, make sure it's fun, easy to participate in, and relevant to your audience.
- **Offer Enticing Rewards**: Prizes should be appealing enough to motivate participation. Consider offering your products or services, exclusive discounts, or even feature winners on your main channels.
- **Promote Widely**: Use all your channels – email, social media, in-store – to promote your contest. The more people know about it, the more content you'll generate.

Showcasing Customer Experiences on Your Platforms

Leveraging UGC on your platforms not only provides authentic content but also builds trust among your audience.

- **Create a Dedicated Section**: Whether on your website, in your newsletter, or on social media, have a specific place where you showcase customer experiences. It could be a photo gallery, a series of testimonials, or a weekly customer spotlight.
- **Tell a Story**: Don't just post a photo or a quote; weave it into a narrative. Share how the customer interacted with your product or

service, what they loved about it, and why it matters.

- **Engage with the Content**: Respond to, like, and share user-generated content. Engagement encourages more sharing and shows customers that their contributions are valued.

In the game of content marketing, user-generated content is like a trump card. It's authentic, relatable, and serves as social proof of your brand's value and appeal.

Leveraging user-generated content is a strategy that combines authenticity with marketing savvy. It's about turning your customers into your storytellers and their experiences into your brand's narrative. As you employ these strategies, remember that the key is to celebrate and amplify these voices. In doing so, you not only enhance your content strategy but also deepen the connection with your audience, building a community around your brand that is engaged, loyal, and vocal.

utilizing traditional marketing techniques

. . .

Old School Tactics, New School Impact –
Bridging the Marketing Gap

Blending Worlds: The Symbiosis of Traditional and Digital Marketing in Today's Era

IN AN AGE where digital platforms dominate the marketing landscape, the enduring power of traditional marketing often seems like a forgotten art. Yet, in the bustling marketplace of the 21st century, the fusion of digital prowess and traditional tactics creates a symphony of marketing effectiveness. This chapter is dedicated to exploring the relevance of traditional marketing in the digital age, uncovering the balance between old-school methods and digital strategies, identifying timeless traditional techniques, and mastering the art of tailoring messages for different mediums.

Balancing Digital and Traditional Marketing Strategies

Imagine marketing as a duet between a classic piano and a modern synthesizer. Both bring unique sounds to the table, and when played together, they create a harmony that's both nostalgic and forward-thinking.

- **Identifying the Strengths of Each Approach**: Understand the unique benefits of digital and traditional marketing. Digital excels in targeting and analytics, while traditional builds brand credibility and broader reach.
- **Creating a Cohesive Strategy**: Integrate digital and traditional marketing in a way that they complement rather than compete with each other. A billboard and a social media campaign can tell parts of the same story.

- **Adapting to Audience Preferences**:
  Different demographics respond differently.
  While millennials might be hooked to digital
  content, baby boomers might resonate more
  with traditional media.

Identifying Effective Traditional Marketing Techniques

Traditional marketing techniques are like the classic hits
of marketing; they never really go out of style. They just
need the right audience and the right moment.

- **Leveraging Print Media**: Newspapers and
  magazines still hold sway in certain
  demographics. Tailored, well-placed ads in these
  mediums can capture a significant audience.
- **Broadcast Media**: Radio and television
  continue to be effective for reaching a wide
  audience, especially for local businesses.
- **Direct Mail**: There's something about a
  tangible piece of mail that digital
  communication can't replicate. It's personal and
  has a tactile impact.

Tailoring Messages for Different Mediums

Each marketing medium speaks its own language. The
key is to tailor your message to fit the medium while maintaining your brand voice.

- **Context is King**: A message that works on a
  billboard may not work in a tweet. Understand

the context and constraints of each medium.
- **Consistency in Branding**: While the message may change, your brand's core identity should remain consistent across all platforms.
- **Feedback and Adaptation**: Use feedback from each medium to refine and adapt your messaging. What works in a print ad might give insights for your digital content.

In the digital age, traditional marketing is not obsolete; it's an essential part of a comprehensive marketing strategy. It's about finding the right mix, the right rhythm in the symphony of your marketing efforts.

As marketing guru Philip Kotler says, "The best advertising is done by satisfied customers." This rings true whether your strategy is digital, traditional, or a blend of both. Satisfied customers are the chorus that amplifies your marketing efforts across all platforms.

Understanding the relevance of traditional marketing in the digital age is about embracing the new without forgetting the old. It's about recognizing that in the tapestry of marketing, both digital and traditional threads have their place. As you navigate through this chapter, you'll learn to weave these threads together, creating a marketing strategy that's robust, versatile, and resonant with your diverse audience. This balanced approach is not just about staying relevant; it's about creating a marketing narrative that's rich, multi-dimensional, and deeply engaging.

Mastering Media Relations: A Guide to Elevating Your Local Business Profile

In a world where digital marketing often steals the spotlight, the enduring charm and effectiveness of engaging local media and press can be a game-changer for businesses, especially for those hosting unique events like trivia nights. This segment focuses on crafting compelling press releases, building relationships with local journalists, and organizing press-invited trivia events, all of which can significantly enhance your business's local presence and appeal.

Crafting Press Releases for Trivia Nights

A well-crafted press release for your trivia night is like sending out an irresistible invitation to a great party. It's not just about the facts; it's about capturing the excitement and uniqueness of your event.

- **Grab Attention with a Catchy Headline**: Your headline should be as catchy as a hit song's chorus. It needs to grab the reader's attention and make them want to know more.
- **Convey the Unique Selling Points**: Highlight what makes your trivia night stand out. Is it the theme, the prizes, or a special guest host?
- **Make it Easy to Digest**: Keep it concise, engaging, and to the point. Journalists are busy; make their job easy.

Building Relationships with Local Journalists

Local journalists are the storytellers of your community, and building a relationship with them can be incredibly beneficial.

- **Understand Their Needs**: Journalists are always looking for interesting stories. Provide them with content that aligns with their audience's interests.
- **Be a Reliable Source**: Consistency and reliability go a long way. Be timely in your responses and keep your promises.
- **Personalize Your Approach**: Get to know the journalists. Understand their beats and preferences. A personalized approach can turn a cold pitch into a warm conversation.

Organizing Press-Invited Trivia Events

Hosting a trivia night where the press is invited is an excellent opportunity to showcase the vibe and energy of your business.

- **Create an Experience**: Make the event memorable. Offer a unique experience that the press would be excited to cover.
- **Provide Exclusive Access**: Give the press exclusive interviews or behind-the-scenes tours. Make them feel special.
- **Follow Up Post-Event**: After the event, follow up with a thank you note and provide additional information or photos they might need for their stories.

In leveraging the power of local media, remember, it's not just about getting your name out there; it's about creating a narrative around your business that resonates with the local community.

Engaging local media and press effectively is akin to weaving a captivating story where your business is the protagonist. It's about creating a narrative so engaging that local journalists are not just observers but become part of the story, helping to amplify your message and connect with the community on a deeper level.

Mastering the art of media relations is a vital skill in the toolbox of any business, especially in an era where local businesses need to stand out more than ever. From crafting captivating press releases for your trivia nights to building meaningful relationships with journalists and organizing events that make headlines, these strategies are about more than just publicity; they're about becoming a valued and recognized part of your local community. As you embark on this journey, let these insights guide you in creating a buzz around your business that resonates with both the media and your audience, propelling your business to new heights of recognition and success.

Reviving the Classics: The Unmatched Power of Flyers, Posters, and Local Ads

In an age dominated by digital noise, the classic charm of flyers, posters, and local advertising stands out like a beacon of simplicity and effectiveness. This segment dives into the art of designing eye-catching promotional materials, the strategic placement of advertisements in high-traffic areas, and the savvy of collaborating with local businesses for cross-promotion. These time-honored techniques, when done right, can create a tangible connection with your audience that many digital strategies struggle to achieve.

Designing Eye-Catching Promotional Materials

The design of your promotional materials is your silent ambassador, speaking volumes about your brand.

- **Keep It Simple but Significant**: Your design should be clear, uncluttered, and easily readable, yet compelling enough to catch the eye and pique interest.
- **Brand Consistency**: Ensure that your materials align with your brand's color scheme, fonts, and overall aesthetic. Consistency builds recognition and trust.
- **Call to Action**: Every piece should have a clear call to action, guiding the viewer on what to do next - whether it's visiting your store, attending an event, or taking advantage of a special offer.

Strategically Placing Advertisements in High-Traffic Areas

Location is as crucial in advertising as it is in real estate. Placing your ads in high-traffic areas ensures maximum visibility.

- **Identify Key Locations**: Scout for places frequented by your target audience. These could be local cafes, community centers, or popular street corners.
- **Consider the Viewer's Journey**: Place your ads where they have the highest chance of being noticed and read - at eye level, near waiting areas, or along paths where people walk regularly.

- **Permission and Legality**: Always ensure you have the necessary permissions for public placements and that your advertisements comply with local regulations.

Collaborating with Local Businesses for Cross-Promotion

Cross-promotion with local businesses creates a symbiotic relationship that can amplify your reach.

- **Identify Synergistic Partners**: Look for businesses that complement yours. For example, a bookstore might partner with a local coffee shop.
- **Mutually Beneficial Offers**: Develop offers that benefit both businesses and the customers. It could be package deals, discounts for mutual customers, or joint events.
- **Share Each Other's Spaces**: Utilize each other's physical and digital spaces for promotions. Display each other's flyers, or give shoutouts on social media.

Incorporating these traditional marketing techniques into your strategy brings a human touch often missing in digital campaigns. It's about creating a physical connection in a digital world.

As marketing pioneer Philip Kotler said, "Marketing is not the art of finding clever ways to dispose of what you make. It is the art of creating genuine customer value." Flyers, posters, and local advertising embody this principle by creating a direct, tangible link between your business and your customers.

The resurgence of traditional marketing methods like flyers, posters, and local ads in the digital age is a testament to their enduring effectiveness. These tools, when used creatively and strategically, can complement your digital efforts, creating a well-rounded marketing strategy that resonates with a diverse audience. As you explore these methods, remember that the goal is to create not just visibility but a memorable and engaging experience for your audience. Through thoughtful design, strategic placement, and collaborative cross-promotion, you can turn these classic marketing tools into powerful conduits for business growth and community engagement.

optimizing your online presence

. . .

Digital Dominance – Crafting an Irresistible
Online Persona

Optimizing Your Online Presence: The Key to a Successful Trivia Night

IN A DIGITAL WORLD where every click counts, optimizing your website for trivia night is like setting the stage for a blockbuster show. It's about creating an online space that not only captivates and informs but also effortlessly guides your visitors towards becoming enthusiastic participants. This chapter is an exploration into the art of crafting a dedicated trivia night page, implementing savvy SEO strategies for local visibility, and ensuring your website's mobile-friendliness and fast load times, all crucial elements in making your trivia night the talk of the town.

Creating a Dedicated Trivia Night Page

Your trivia night page is your virtual billboard, an inviting glimpse into the fun and excitement that awaits your visitors.

- **Clarity and Appeal**: Design your page to be visually appealing and easy to navigate. Use clear, concise language and enticing imagery that resonates with the trivia night theme.
- **Up-to-Date Information**: Keep your trivia night schedule, themes, rules, and prizes up-to-date. This not only helps in planning for your visitors but also reflects the vibrancy and dynamism of your events.
- **Call to Action**: Include a strong call to action - whether it's to book a table, sign up for a trivia team, or subscribe for updates. Make the next steps clear and easy.

Implementing SEO Strategies for Local Visibility

In the vast ocean of the internet, SEO is your beacon that guides local trivia enthusiasts to your website.

- **Local Keywords**: Use local SEO strategies by incorporating location-specific keywords into your content. This could include your city, neighborhood, or even popular local landmarks.
- **Google My Business**: Optimize your Google My Business listing with up-to-date information, photos, and posts about your trivia nights. This enhances your visibility in local search results.
- **Engaging Content**: Regularly update your blog or news section with engaging content about your trivia nights. Share fun facts, trivia leaderboards, or recaps of past events to keep the content fresh and engaging.

Ensuring Mobile-Friendliness and Fast Load Times

With most users accessing websites through their mobile devices, having a mobile-friendly website with fast loading times is non-negotiable.

- **Responsive Design**: Ensure your website has a responsive design that adjusts seamlessly to different screen sizes, providing an optimal browsing experience on both desktops and mobile devices.
- **Optimize Images and Videos**: Large images and videos can slow down your site. Optimize

them for quicker loading times without compromising on quality.

- **Regular Website Audits**: Conduct regular website audits to identify and fix any issues that might be slowing down your site, ensuring a smooth and fast user experience.

In this digital age, a well-optimized website is a powerful tool in your marketing arsenal. It's the first point of contact many potential customers will have with your trivia night, and you want to make a lasting impression.

As marketing guru Seth Godin once said, "Marketing is no longer about the stuff you make, but about the stories you tell." Your website is where these stories begin. It's where curiosity is piqued, plans are made, and anticipation builds.

In conclusion, optimizing your website for trivia night is about more than just aesthetics and functionality. It's about creating an online experience that mirrors the excitement and engagement of your actual event. It's about weaving a digital narrative that draws visitors in and leaves them eager to experience the real thing. As you embark on this journey of website optimization, remember, your goal is to not just inform but to enchant, not just to list details but to build anticipation, turning casual browsers into dedicated trivia night attendees.

SEO Strategies for Trivia Night Success: Boosting Visibility in the Digital Realm

In the bustling digital world, harnessing the power of Search Engine Optimization (SEO) can transform your trivia night from a hidden gem to the talk of the town. This chapter delves into the nuances of effective SEO practices, focusing on keyword research for trivia-related content, local SEO tactics for bars and restaurants, and the importance of regularly updating content for sustained relevance and freshness.

Keyword Research for Trivia-Related Content

Navigating the world of SEO starts with understanding the power of keywords. For trivia nights, it's about finding the sweet spot between common search terms and those unique to your offerings.

- **Identify Relevant Keywords**: Use tools like Google Keyword Planner or SEMrush to find keywords related to trivia, such as "trivia night near me" or "best trivia questions."
- **Analyze Search Intent**: Understand why someone would search for these keywords. Are they looking for a fun night out, trivia questions, or a local competition?
- **Incorporate Keywords Naturally**: Sprinkle these keywords throughout your website content, blog posts, and trivia night descriptions in a way that feels natural and engaging.

Local SEO Tactics for Bars and Restaurants

For bars and restaurants hosting trivia nights, local SEO is the cornerstone of your digital strategy.

- **Google My Business Optimization**: Ensure your Google My Business listing is complete and up-to-date, with accurate hours, location, and trivia night schedules.

- **Local Keywords**: Include location-based keywords in your website's metadata, headers, and content to rank higher in local search results.
- **Engage in Local Link Building**: Establish links from local directories, community websites, and other local businesses to boost your visibility in local search results.

Regularly Updating Content for Freshness and Relevance

The digital world is ever-evolving, and your website content should reflect this dynamism. Regular updates not only keep your website fresh but also signal to search engines that your site is a relevant source of information.

- **Blog About Trivia Topics**: Maintain a blog where you post about trivia-related topics, upcoming events, or recaps of past nights. This keeps your content fresh and engaging.
- **Update Event Pages**: Regularly update your trivia night pages with new themes, questions, or special events to keep visitors coming back for more.
- **Encourage User Interaction**: User-generated content, such as reviews or comments, can keep your website content dynamic and engaging.

SEO for trivia nights is not just about climbing the

search engine rankings; it's about connecting with a community that shares your passion for trivia.

As digital marketing expert Neil Patel says, "SEO is not about gaming the system anymore; it's about learning how to play by the rules." This approach is especially true for trivia nights, where success lies in understanding and appealing to your audience's interests and search behaviors.

Mastering SEO for your trivia night is a blend of art and science. It involves understanding your audience, using the right tools to research keywords, optimizing your local presence, and keeping your content fresh and engaging. As you navigate through this chapter, remember that the goal is to not just attract traffic but to build a community of trivia enthusiasts who are excited about what you have to offer. By leveraging SEO effectively, you can turn your trivia night into a bustling hub of activity, drawing in both dedicated trivia aficionados and curious newcomers alike.

Crafting a Digital Buzz: The Art of Blogging and Multimedia Content for Trivia Nights

In the digital age, engaging your audience through blogging and multimedia content is not just an option; it's an essential strategy to bring your trivia nights into the spotlight. This segment of the chapter explores the dynamic world of digital content creation, from writing compelling blog posts about your trivia nights, harnessing the power of multimedia like videos and podcasts, to the strategic collaboration with influencers and guest bloggers. These tools, when used effectively, can turn your trivia night from a local event into a digital sensation.

Writing Compelling Blog Posts About Trivia Nights

Your blog is the storytelling platform for your trivia nights. It's where the excitement, knowledge, and community spirit of your events come alive in words.

- **Share Behind-the-Scenes Stories**: Give your readers a peek behind the curtain. Share the process of setting up trivia nights, selecting questions, or even fun anecdotes from past events.
- **Offer Valuable Insights**: Post articles that offer tips on trivia strategies, interesting facts, or highlight unique trivia themes. This type of content positions you as a thought leader in the trivia community.
- **Engage with Your Readers**: End your posts with questions or calls to action that encourage reader interaction. Engagement boosts your blog's visibility and creates a community around your content.

Utilizing Multimedia Content (Videos, Podcasts)

In a world where content is consumed in various formats, diversifying into multimedia can significantly enhance your reach and engagement.

- **Create Engaging Videos**: Post videos of trivia night highlights, participant interviews, or even question teasers. Videos are shareable and can quickly capture the essence of your events.
- **Start a Trivia Podcast**: Launch a podcast where you discuss trivia topics, interview trivia enthusiasts, or even host a virtual trivia session.

Podcasts can tap into a different audience segment and build a loyal listener base.

- **Consistency is Key**: Whether it's videos or podcasts, maintain a consistent posting schedule. Regular uploads keep your audience engaged and looking forward to more content.

Collaborating with Influencers and Guest Bloggers

Collaboration with influencers and guest bloggers can infuse new perspectives into your content and broaden your reach.

- **Identify the Right Collaborators**: Look for influencers or bloggers who align with your brand and have an engaged audience. Their endorsement can lend credibility and attract their followers to your trivia nights.
- **Co-create Content**: Work together on content creation. This could be a guest post on your blog, a co-hosted trivia night, or a joint video or podcast episode.
- **Leverage Each Other's Platforms**: Use the collaboration as an opportunity to cross-promote each other. Share each other's content on your respective platforms to maximize reach.

Engaging through blogging and multimedia content is like weaving a rich tapestry of stories, experiences, and interactions around your trivia nights. It's a strategy that not only markets your events but also builds a digital community of trivia lovers.

The journey of blogging and content creation for trivia

nights is an exciting blend of storytelling, creativity, and community building. As you embark on this journey, remember that the goal is to not just inform but to captivate, engage, and create a sense of community around your brand. Through well-crafted blog posts, diverse multimedia content, and strategic collaborations, you can transform your trivia nights into a digital phenomenon, drawing trivia enthusiasts not just to your website but to your venue.

crafting engaging promotions and offers

. . .

Irresistible Deals – Designing Offers They Can't Refuse

Decoding Customer Choices: The Art of Influencing Decisions in the Trivia Night Scene

UNDERSTANDING what drives customer decisions in today's market is akin to being a mind reader at a trivia night - it requires insight, understanding, and a bit of strategic thinking. In this chapter, we delve into the psychology behind customer preferences and behaviors, particularly in the context of organizing and promoting trivia nights. We'll explore how to create tailored promotions for different audience segments and balance profitability with attractiveness in offers, ensuring your trivia night not only captivates but also converts interest into action.

Analyzing Customer Preferences and Behaviors

Every customer is a story, and understanding their preferences is like reading the first chapter of their narrative.

Gather Data: Utilize surveys, feedback forms, and social media interactions to gather data about your customers. What are their interests, age demographics, and what drives them to participate in trivia nights?

Observe Trends: Pay attention to trends in customer behavior. Which trivia themes get the most attendance? What time slots are most popular? This information is gold in tailoring your future events.

Feedback Analysis: Regularly analyze feedback. What are customers saying about your trivia nights? Use this information to fine-tune the experience.

Creating Tailored Promotions for Different Audience Segments

Not all trivia buffs are cut from the same cloth. Tailoring your promotions to different audience segments can significantly increase your appeal.

Segment Your Audience: Break down your audience into segments - college students, working professionals, trivia enthusiasts, etc. Understand what each segment values in a trivia night.

Customized Offers: Create offers that appeal to each segment. Students might appreciate a discount night, while professionals might be attracted to networking opportunities during trivia.

Targeted Advertising: Use targeted advertising on social media and other platforms to reach each segment effectively. Tailor your message to resonate with each group's interests and preferences.

Balancing Profitability and Attractiveness in Offers

Finding the sweet spot between profitability and offer attractiveness is like balancing a scale – it takes precision and understanding.

Analyze Costs and Benefits: Understand the cost of your offers and balance them against the potential benefits. Profitability doesn't always mean cutting costs; sometimes, it's about creating more value.

Attractive Pricing Strategies: Implement pricing strategies that are attractive to your customers but also maintain a healthy bottom line. Consider tiered pricing, special packages, or loyalty discounts.

Monitor and Adjust: Regularly monitor the performance of your offers. Are they attracting customers? Are they profitable? Use this data to make informed adjustments.

Understanding customer decisions in the realm of trivia nights is about more than just filling seats; it's about creating experiences that resonate with your target audience, encouraging repeat visits and word-of-mouth promotion.

As marketing guru Philip Kotler said, "The best advertising is done by satisfied customers." Satisfied customers are the result of understanding and meeting their needs and preferences, which is the essence of this chapter.

In conclusion, understanding what drives customer decisions is a crucial component in the successful organization and promotion of trivia nights. By analyzing customer preferences, creating tailored promotions, and balancing profitability with offer attractiveness, you can develop a deep connection with your audience. This connection is the key to not only drawing customers in but also building a loyal community around your trivia nights. As you dive deeper into this chapter, remember, your goal is to not just understand your customers but to anticipate their needs and exceed their expectations, turning your trivia night into the must-attend event in town.

Unleashing Creativity in Trivia Nights: The Magic of Themed Events

In the world of trivia, themes are more than just dressing – they're the soul of the party. Designing themed trivia nights is an art form, transforming a regular quiz session into an immersive experience that captures the imagination and hearts of your audience. This segment delves into creating unique and memorable themes, effectively tying in promotions, and using them to attract specific demographics, turning your trivia nights into must-attend events.

Creating Unique and Memorable Themes

The theme of your trivia night is the first hook that catches your audience's interest. It sets the stage for an engaging experience.

- **Brainstorming Original Ideas**: Look beyond the usual suspects like movie or sports themes. Think about current trends, historical eras, or even fantasy worlds. The key is originality and fun.
- **Interactive Elements**: Incorporate interactive elements that align with your theme. If it's a '90s night, think about including a mini dance-off to '90s hits between rounds.
- **Consistency Across the Board**: Ensure that everything from the questions to the decorations and staff attire aligns with the theme to create a truly immersive experience.

Tying in Promotions with Themes

Promotions tied to your themes not only boost attendance but also enhance the overall experience of your trivia night.

- **Themed Discounts and Offers**: Offer discounts or special deals that relate to your theme. For example, a 'Superhero Night' could include discounts for guests dressed as their favorite superheroes.
- **Social Media Tie-ins**: Use your theme to create engaging social media posts and contests that build anticipation and engagement before the event.

- **Themed Prizes**: Align your prizes with the theme of the night. It adds an extra layer of excitement and gives participants another reason to dive into the theme.

Utilizing Themes to Attract Specific Demographics

Themes can be a powerful tool to target specific groups of people, tailoring your trivia night to their interests and preferences.

- **Research Your Audience**: Understanding the demographics of your regular patrons or the audience you want to attract is key. What are their interests? What age group are they in?
- **Themed Nights for Different Groups**: Host different themed nights that appeal to various groups. A 'Pop Culture Night' might attract a younger crowd, while a 'Classic Rock Night' could be a hit with an older demographic.
- **Feedback and Adaptation**: After each themed night, gather feedback. What did your audience enjoy? What could be improved? Use this to refine your future themes.

The art of designing themed trivia nights is about creating a memorable experience that goes beyond just answering questions. It's about crafting a night that transports your guests into different worlds, leaving them with stories to tell and experiences to share.

As Walt Disney famously said, "Do what you do so well that they will want to see it again and bring their friends."

This is the essence of a successful themed trivia night. Create an experience so captivating that your guests not only come back for more but also bring others along.

Themed trivia nights are an opportunity to showcase creativity, engage your audience on a deeper level, and create an atmosphere that buzzes with excitement and anticipation. By thoughtfully crafting themes, aligning promotions, and targeting specific demographics, you transform trivia nights from a simple game of questions and answers into an unforgettable social experience. As you explore the boundless possibilities of themed events, remember, your goal is to not just host a trivia night but to create an experience that resonates, delights, and brings people together in the spirit of fun and camaraderie.

Captivating the Crowd: Mastering Time-Sensitive Offers for Maximum Engagement

In the fast-paced world of dining and entertainment, time-sensitive offers and specials are like the secret spices that make a dish irresistible. They create a sense of urgency, add excitement, and encourage customers to act fast. This segment of our chapter dives into the art of designing these compelling, limited-time offers, using special events and holidays for themed promotions, and importantly, measuring their impact to fine-tune future strategies for your trivia nights.

Designing Limited-Time Offers to Create Urgency

The key to a successful limited-time offer is creating a sense of urgency without sacrificing the quality or perception of the service.

- **Clear Time Frame**: Define a clear start and end date for your offers. This clarity not only adds to the urgency but also makes it easier for customers to plan.
- **Attractive Deals**: The offer should be compelling enough to act as an immediate draw. Whether it's a discount, a special menu, or exclusive access, make it irresistible.
- **Effective Promotion**: Utilize all your channels – social media, email newsletters, your website, and in-house advertising – to promote these time-sensitive offers. The goal is to reach as many potential customers as quickly as possible.

Using Special Events and Holidays for Themed Promotions

Special events and holidays provide a perfect opportunity to introduce themed promotions, adding a festive or unique twist to your trivia nights.

- **Calendar-Based Planning**: Plan your themed promotions around popular holidays and events. Whether it's a Halloween Spooktacular trivia night or a Valentine's Day couples' quiz, aligning with these dates can attract more participants.
- **Themed Offerings**: Align your offers with the theme. For instance, a Christmas-themed trivia night could feature holiday-inspired cocktails or a special festive menu.

- **Engaging Marketing**: Use themed visuals and language in your marketing materials. Create an atmosphere that begins with the first point of contact, be it a social media post or a flyer.

Measuring the Impact and Tweaking Future Offers

Understanding the effectiveness of your offers is crucial in crafting even more successful future promotions.

- **Track Participation and Sales**: Use your POS system and registration data to track how many customers are taking advantage of your offers and their spending patterns.
- **Customer Feedback**: Directly ask your customers what they thought of the event and the offer. This can be done through feedback forms, social media polls, or informal conversations.
- **Analyze and Adapt**: Use the data you've collected to analyze what worked and what didn't. Was the offer too generous, cutting into profits? Was the theme not as engaging as expected? Use these insights to refine your future offers.

Creating time-sensitive offers and specials for trivia nights is not just a promotional tactic; it's about creating memorable experiences that customers look forward to and talk about long after they're over.

Mastering time-sensitive offers for your trivia nights is

an art that involves a delicate balance of urgency, appeal, and strategic timing. It's about understanding your customers, what excites them, and how to make your offers stand out in a crowded market. As you venture further into this chapter, keep in mind that the goal is to not only attract customers with these offers but to create an experience that keeps them coming back for more, time and time again. Through careful planning, creative theming, and diligent analysis, you can turn your trivia nights into eagerly anticipated events that consistently draw a crowd.

engaging the community through events

. . .

Beyond Trivia – Creating a Community Hub

Elevating Your Venue: The Art of Planning and Hosting Special Events

WHEN IT COMES to hosting special events, especially in the dynamic world of trivia nights, it's about much more than just putting together a list of questions. It's about creating experiences that linger in the memory, turning your venue into a hub of excitement and entertainment. This chapter unveils the secrets to conceptualizing events that go beyond the ordinary, partnering with local groups to enrich the experience, and crafting an event calendar that keeps your audience engaged and returning for more.

Conceptualizing Events Beyond Regular Trivia Nights

Special events should feel like an adventure, a departure from the routine that invigorates your regular patrons and attracts new faces.

- **Thematic Innovation**: Think outside the box with themes. Go beyond the usual and dive into less explored territories - be it a night dedicated to obscure 80s pop culture or an evening exploring the wonders of the animal kingdom.
- **Interactive Elements**: Add interactive components to your events. This could mean live performances, themed quizzes, or interactive apps that complement the trivia experience.
- **Feedback-Driven Ideas**: Listen to your audience. What themes excite them? What special events would they love to see? This

feedback is invaluable in shaping unique event concepts.

Partnering with Local Groups and Societies

Collaboration can add layers of richness and authenticity to your events, making them stand out in a crowded market.

- **Identify Potential Partners**: Local hobby groups, societies, or even other businesses can bring new dimensions to your events. A partnership with a local brewery, for example, can turn a regular trivia night into a craft beer tasting extravaganza.
- **Mutual Promotion**: Work together on promoting the event. It's a win-win situation – you get to tap into their audience base, and they get to showcase their products or services to your patrons.
- **Create a Community Feel**: Collaborations can help foster a sense of community. They show your commitment to local businesses and groups, which resonates well with today's socially conscious consumers.

Creating an Event Calendar and Promoting Consistently

A well-planned event calendar is your roadmap to a year filled with exciting, engaging, and memorable experiences.

- **Strategic Planning**: Map out your events for the year. Consider seasonality, local holidays, and significant events in your community. This helps in creating a diverse and engaging calendar.
- **Consistent Promotion**: Use a mix of digital and traditional marketing to promote your events. Social media, email newsletters, in-house advertising, and local media can all play a role in spreading the word.
- **Early Bird Teasers**: Start promoting early with teasers and sneak peeks. It builds anticipation and gives your audience something to look forward to.

Planning and hosting special events are about creating a buzz, an excitement that makes your venue the go-to place in town.

As event planning expert Judy Allen puts it, "The most successful events are the ones that achieve your goals and exceed your expectations." This is what you should aim for with each event you plan and host.

This chapter is your guide to transforming your trivia nights into a series of special events that captivate and delight your audience. It's about understanding the pulse of your community, embracing creativity in your concepts, and building partnerships that enrich the experience. As you delve deeper, remember, the goal is to create events that are not just successful in terms of turnout but memorable in terms of experience, leaving your guests eagerly awaiting your next big event.

Cultivating Community Spirit: The Heart of Successful Event Planning

In the bustling realm of bars and restaurants, involving the community in event planning is not just a strategy; it's the heartbeat that keeps your establishment alive and pulsating with energy. This segment of the chapter explores the transformative power of soliciting ideas and feedback from patrons, hosting community-focused events, and building a loyal community around your venue. It's about turning customers into collaborators, co-creators, and, ultimately, champions of your brand.

Soliciting Ideas and Feedback from Patrons

Your patrons are your most valuable resource when it comes to understanding what makes an event successful.

- **Open Channels for Feedback**: Create easy and accessible ways for your patrons to share their ideas and feedback. This could be through suggestion boxes, social media polls, or informal chats.
- **Host Brainstorming Sessions**: Consider hosting informal gatherings where regulars can pitch ideas for events. It's a great way to foster a sense of ownership and community.
- **Act on Feedback**: Show your patrons that their input is valued by acting on feasible ideas. This not only improves your events but also strengthens patron loyalty.

Hosting Community-Focused Events

Events that resonate with the local community's spirit can turn your establishment into more than just a venue – it becomes a gathering place.

- **Identify Community Interests**: Understand the interests and passions of your community. Is there a local sports team everyone supports? Are there local causes that they care deeply about?
- **Partner with Local Groups**: Collaborate with local organizations or charities to host events. This not only brings new patrons into your establishment but also contributes positively to your community.
- **Create Signature Community Events**: Develop events that could become a staple in your community's calendar, like an annual charity trivia night or a local talent showcase.

Building a Community Around Your Bar or Restaurant

A strong community is the foundation of any successful establishment in the hospitality industry.

- **Foster Regular Patronage**: Encourage regular visits through loyalty programs or special perks for locals. Regular patrons are the core of your community.
- **Engage Beyond the Bar**: Connect with your patrons outside of business hours through social media, newsletters, or community forums. Share updates, stories, or fun trivia related to your events.

- **Create a Welcoming Atmosphere**: Ensure
  that your establishment is not just a place to eat
  and drink, but a space where everyone feels
  welcome and valued. A friendly and inclusive
  atmosphere is key to building a strong
  community.

Involving the community in your event planning is about creating experiences that are not just enjoyed but cherished. It's about transforming your establishment from a mere venue to a beloved community landmark.

This chapter is a guide to harnessing the power of community in event planning. It's about understanding that your patrons are more than customers; they are a part of your extended family. By actively involving them in your event planning, hosting community-focused events, and nurturing a welcoming atmosphere, you can create a sense of belonging that turns first-time visitors into regulars and regulars into advocates. As you move forward, remember that the strength of your events lies not just in their execution but in the community spirit they embody and foster.

Maximizing Marketing Impact: Transforming Events into Powerful Promotional Tools

In the vibrant world of bars and restaurants, events are not just gatherings; they are potent marketing tools. Leveraging events for marketing is akin to casting a wider net in the ocean of potential patrons. This segment focuses on the strategic use of events to gather valuable customer data, cross-promote trivia nights, and create captivating event-based marketing content. It's about turning each event into a golden opportunity to boost your brand's visibility and appeal.

Using Events to Gather Customer Data

Information is power in the business world, and events are a treasure trove of customer data waiting to be unlocked.

- **Registration and Feedback Forms**: Use registration forms for events and post-event feedback surveys. They can provide insights into customer preferences and demographics.
- **Social Media Engagement**: Monitor social media interactions during events. Which posts are getting the most attention? What are people saying about your event?
- **Analyzing Data for Future Strategies**: Use the data gathered to tailor future events, menu offerings, and marketing strategies. Understanding your customer base is key to business growth.

Cross-Promoting Trivia Nights at Other Events

Cross-promotion is a savvy strategy to maximize your event's marketing potential.

- **Incorporate Trivia Elements in Other Events**: If you're hosting a live music night or a special dinner, include a mini-trivia session. It's a great way to introduce guests to your trivia nights.

- **Use Events as Teasers**: Give a sneak peek of upcoming trivia themes or special rounds during other events. It builds anticipation and interest.
- **Offer Special Deals**: Provide exclusive offers or discounts for your trivia nights to attendees of other events. This can encourage them to come back for your trivia nights.

Creating Event-Based Marketing Content

In today's digital age, content is king, and events are a gold mine for content creation.

- **Capture the Event**: Create engaging videos or photo albums showcasing the highlights of your events. This visual content can be shared across various platforms, attracting a wider audience.
- **Blogging About Events**: Write blog posts detailing the event experience, special moments, or behind-the-scenes stories. These posts can humanize your brand and create a deeper connection with your audience.
- **Leverage Testimonials and Reviews**: Encourage attendees to share their experiences on social media or review platforms. Authentic testimonials can be powerful marketing tools.

Events, when leveraged correctly, can significantly amplify your marketing efforts. They offer a unique opportunity to engage with your customers in a personal and memorable way.

As marketing expert Jay Baer says, "If your stories are all about your products and services, that's not storytelling.

It's a brochure. Give yourself permission to make the story bigger." This is particularly relevant when it comes to event marketing. It's not just about promoting a product or service; it's about creating a narrative that resonates with your audience.

It's about understanding the multifaceted role events can play in not only bringing people together but also in gathering valuable data, cross-promoting your offerings, and generating engaging content. As you explore these strategies, remember, the goal is to create a seamless blend of entertainment and marketing, one that not only celebrates your brand but also resonates with and captivates your audience. With the right approach, every event you host can become a stepping stone towards building a stronger, more vibrant brand presence.

analytics and feedback – measuring success and improving

. . .

Data-Driven Decisions – The Key to Continuous Growth

Demystifying Marketing Analytics: A Roadmap for Data-Driven Success

IN TODAY'S DIGITAL AGE, understanding and utilizing marketing analytics is like having a GPS for your business journey. It provides the data-driven insight needed to navigate the complex world of marketing, ensuring every decision you make is informed and impactful. This chapter is a deep dive into the world of marketing analytics, focusing on tracking and analyzing your marketing efforts, utilizing the latest tools and software for data analysis, and adapting your strategies based on performance metrics. It's designed to transform data into your most powerful ally in the competitive world of trivia night hosting.

Tracking and Analyzing Marketing Efforts

The first step in harnessing the power of marketing analytics is to track and analyze your efforts meticulously.

- **Identify Key Metrics**: Understand which metrics are most relevant to your goals. Is it website traffic, social media engagement, or event attendance rates?
- **Use Analytics Tools**: Employ tools like Google Analytics or social media insights to track these metrics. Understanding your audience's behavior online can provide invaluable insights.
- **Regular Reviews**: Make it a routine to review your analytics. This ongoing process helps you understand trends, patterns, and the impact of your marketing efforts.

Utilizing Tools and Software for Data Analysis

In a world brimming with data, the right tools and software can make all the difference.

- **Choosing the Right Tools**: Select tools that align with your business needs and objectives. Whether it's social media analytics tools, email marketing software, or customer relationship management systems, the right tool can offer deep insights.
- **Integrating Various Data Sources**: Ensure that your tools can integrate data from various sources for a holistic view. This integrated approach can reveal more comprehensive insights.
- **Training and Expertise**: Invest in training for yourself and your team to make the most of these tools. Understanding how to interpret data is crucial.

Adapting Strategies Based on Performance Metrics

The ultimate goal of marketing analytics is to adapt and refine your strategies for maximum effectiveness.

- **Data-Driven Decisions**: Let your data guide your decisions. If analytics show that certain types of events or promotions are more successful, focus your efforts in those areas.
- **Testing and Experimenting**: Use data to test different approaches. Try different types of

event themes or marketing messages and measure the results.

- **Continuous Improvement**: View the use of marketing analytics as a journey, not a destination. There's always room for improvement and growth.

Understanding and utilizing marketing analytics is like having a conversation with your audience at scale. It's about listening to what the data says and responding in a way that resonates with your audience.

In conclusion, this chapter is a guide to turning the often overwhelming world of data into a clear, navigable path towards business growth and success. It's about embracing the power of analytics to not just understand your current standing but to predict and shape future trends. Whether you're a seasoned marketer or just starting, this chapter will provide you with the knowledge and tools to make data-driven decisions that can elevate your trivia night events and transform your marketing approach. Remember, in the world of analytics, every piece of data is a stepping stone towards understanding your audience better and serving them more effectively.

Mastering the Art of Feedback: Transforming Opinions into Business Success

In the dynamic world of trivia night hosting, customer feedback is the compass that guides your ship. Embracing feedback is not just about listening; it's about actively seeking and implementing those suggestions to enhance your events and marketing strategies. This chapter segment delves into the most effective ways to gather feedback, using it to refine your trivia nights and marketing efforts, and finding the sweet spot between customer desires and business objectives. It's a journey towards creating a trivia night experience that resonates with your audience while also aligning with your business goals.

Effective Ways to Gather Feedback

Collecting feedback is an art that, when mastered, can provide invaluable insights into your customers' minds.

- **Digital Surveys**: Utilize digital platforms to send out post-event surveys. Make them short, engaging, and easy to complete.
- **Social Media Engagement**: Use social media platforms to ask direct questions about your events. Polls, open-ended questions, and interactive stories can be effective tools.
- **In-person Conversations**: Sometimes, the best feedback comes from casual conversations. Encourage your staff to chat with patrons and gather their thoughts.

Using Feedback to Improve Trivia Nights and Marketing

Feedback is like a gold mine of ideas to improve your trivia nights and fine-tune your marketing efforts.

- **Event Experience Enhancement**: Use feedback to understand what themes, questions, or formats are most popular. This can help in designing future trivia nights that are more engaging and entertaining.

- **Refining Marketing Messages**: Feedback can also provide insights into what marketing messages resonate with your audience. Tailor your communications based on what your audience finds appealing.
- **Identifying Areas for Improvement**: Look for recurring themes in feedback to identify areas that need improvement. It could be anything from the sound system to the type of questions asked.

Balancing Customer Desires with Business Goals

While customer feedback is crucial, it's also essential to balance these insights with your business objectives.

- **Feasibility Analysis**: Not all feedback can be implemented. Analyze suggestions for their feasibility and alignment with your business goals.
- **Incremental Changes**: Implement changes gradually. This allows you to measure the impact of each change without overwhelming your regular operations.
- **Staying True to Your Brand**: Ensure that the feedback implemented aligns with your brand's identity and values. It's about enhancing your offering, not losing your unique brand essence.

Gathering and implementing customer feedback is a

strategic approach that can lead to a more engaging and successful trivia night experience. It's about creating a two-way conversation with your customers, where their opinions are valued and acted upon.

This chapter segment is your guide to harnessing the power of customer feedback. It's about understanding that each piece of feedback, whether positive or negative, is a stepping stone towards creating a better, more successful trivia night experience. As you explore these strategies, remember that the ultimate goal is to blend customer desires with your business objectives, creating an experience that is not only enjoyable for your patrons but also profitable and sustainable for your business. Through active listening, thoughtful implementation, and a balanced approach, you can turn customer opinions into one of your greatest business assets.

Evolving with Excellence: The Never-Ending Journey of Marketing Mastery

In the ever-changing world of bar and restaurant marketing, embracing a mindset of continuous improvement and adaptation isn't just a strategy; it's a necessity for survival and success. This segment delves into the importance of continuous learning, regularly updating marketing strategies, and staying ahead of market trends and customer preferences. It's about recognizing that the world of marketing, much like a trivia game, is constantly evolving with new questions and challenges, requiring you to always be on your toes, ready to adapt.

Embracing a Mindset of Continuous Learning

In the realm of marketing, stagnation is the enemy. Embracing a mindset of continuous learning is key.

- **Stay Curious**: Always be on the lookout for new ideas, techniques, and strategies. Attend webinars, read industry blogs, and participate in forums.
- **Learn from Mistakes**: View every setback as a learning opportunity. Analyze what went wrong and use those insights to improve.
- **Encourage Team Learning**: Foster a culture of learning within your team. Encourage them to share insights and learn from each other.

Regularly Updating Marketing Strategies

In a world where consumer behaviors and technologies are constantly shifting, regularly updating your marketing strategies is crucial.

- **Review and Revise**: Regularly review your marketing strategies to identify what's working and what isn't. Don't be afraid to revise your approach based on new data and insights.
- **Experiment with New Tactics**: Be open to experimenting with new marketing channels and tactics. What works today might not work tomorrow, so stay flexible and adaptable.
- **Customer Feedback Loop**: Regularly seek customer feedback and integrate it into your marketing strategies. This can help you stay aligned with your audience's evolving needs.

Staying Ahead of Market Trends and Customer Preferences

Staying ahead of the curve is essential in a competitive market.

- **Market Research**: Conduct regular market research to stay updated on industry trends and consumer preferences. This can involve surveys, focus groups, or studying industry reports.
- **Social Listening**: Use social listening tools to monitor what customers are saying about your brand and your competitors online. This can provide real-time insights into consumer attitudes and preferences.
- **Adapt Quickly**: Develop the ability to quickly adapt to changing market conditions. The faster you can respond to new trends, the better you can meet your customers' needs.

Marketing, much like hosting a trivia night, is about engaging your audience in a dynamic and ever-changing environment. It requires creativity, adaptability, and a willingness to learn and evolve continuously.

This segment emphasizes the importance of continuous improvement and adaptation in marketing. It's about being proactive rather than reactive, staying ahead of trends, and consistently refining your strategies to meet the ever-changing demands of the market. Whether you're a seasoned marketing professional or new to the game, this segment offers practical advice and insights to help you navigate the complex and exciting world of marketing.

Remember, the journey of marketing mastery is never-ending, but each step taken on this path can lead to greater success and a deeper connection with your audience.

building a sustainable trivia marketing plan

. . .

Long-Term Success – Crafting a Future-Proof
Strategy

Charting the Future: The Power of Long-Term Planning in Marketing

IN THE WHIRLWIND of daily operations and immediate concerns, the importance of long-term planning in the marketing sphere is often overshadowed. Yet, just like a skilled trivia master who knows the value of a well-prepared question bank, savvy marketers understand the significance of setting achievable long-term goals, balancing short-term tactics with long-term strategies, and preparing for market changes and challenges. This introductory segment lays the foundation for exploring the strategic foresight that's crucial in steering your bar or restaurant's marketing efforts towards sustained success.

Setting Achievable Long-Term Goals

The foundation of any effective long-term plan is setting goals that are ambitious yet achievable.

- **Vision Alignment**: Ensure your long-term goals align with the overall vision of your business. They should be the guiding stars that direct all your marketing efforts.
- **SMART Goals**: Embrace the SMART framework – Specific, Measurable, Achievable, Relevant, and Time-bound – to set clear and attainable goals.
- **Regular Reviews**: Regularly revisit and adjust these goals as your business and the market evolve. Flexibility is key to staying relevant.

Balancing Short-Term Tactics with Long-Term Strategies

The art of marketing lies in striking the perfect balance between short-term wins and long-term vision.

- **Integrated Approach**: Develop a marketing strategy that integrates immediate tactics with long-term plans. Each campaign should contribute to the bigger picture.
- **Resource Allocation**: Wisely allocate resources between immediate needs and long-term investments. This might mean sacrificing short-term gains for long-term growth.
- **Consistency and Patience**: Remember that long-term strategies require consistency and patience. The results might not be immediate, but they will be sustainable.

Preparing for Market Changes and Challenges

In a landscape as dynamic as marketing, being prepared for change is not optional, but mandatory.

- **Stay Informed**: Keep abreast of market trends and shifts. This might involve continual research, attending industry events, or networking with peers.
- **Adaptability**: Cultivate a culture of adaptability in your team. Encourage innovative thinking and flexibility to swiftly respond to market changes.

- **Risk Management**: Have contingency plans in place. This involves anticipating potential challenges and having strategies ready to mitigate risks.

Long-term planning in marketing is akin to planting a tree. The results may not be immediate, but with consistent care and strategic nurturing, it grows into something strong and enduring.

It's about understanding that in the game of marketing, just like in trivia, the winners are those who think ahead, plan meticulously, and adapt swiftly. Whether you're a seasoned marketer or new to the field, the insights provided here will equip you with the knowledge and tools to plan not just for the next event, but for the continued success and growth of your business. Remember, effective long-term planning is not just about predicting the future; it's about creating it.

Harmonizing Your Marketing Symphony: Mastering Multichannel Strategies

Imagine your marketing strategy as a symphony orchestra. Each instrument – or marketing channel – has its unique sound, but it's the harmony and coordination among them that create a mesmerizing performance. This segment explores the art of integrating all marketing channels to create a cohesive strategy, ensuring brand consistency, and leveraging each channel's strengths for maximum impact.

Creating a Cohesive Marketing Strategy Across All Platforms

The cornerstone of effective multichannel marketing is a cohesive strategy that seamlessly integrates all platforms.

- **Unified Vision**: Begin by establishing a unified vision for your marketing campaign. This vision should guide the tone, style, and message across all channels.
- **Integrated Planning**: Develop an integrated marketing plan that outlines how each channel will contribute to the overall strategy. This involves understanding the unique role of each platform.
- **Consistent Messaging**: Ensure that your core message is consistent across all channels. This doesn't mean replicating content verbatim but adapting it to fit the context of each platform.

Ensuring Brand Consistency and Message Alignment

Brand consistency is the glue that holds your multi-channel strategy together.

- **Brand Guidelines**: Develop comprehensive brand guidelines that cover everything from visual elements to tone of voice. This ensures consistency no matter who is creating the content.
- **Cross-Channel Review**: Regularly review content across all channels to ensure alignment with your brand identity and marketing goals.

- **Feedback Loop**: Establish a feedback loop within your team to identify discrepancies in brand representation and rectify them swiftly.

Leveraging Each Channel's Strengths for Maximum Impact

Each marketing channel has its unique strengths. The key is to leverage these to your advantage.

- **Channel Specialization**: Understand the strengths and limitations of each channel. For example, use social media for engagement and storytelling, while email might be more effective for direct offers and calls to action.
- **Target Audience Analysis**: Analyze where your target audience spends their time and what type of content resonates with them on each platform.
- **Synergistic Campaigns**: Create campaigns where channels complement and enhance each other. For instance, a social media teaser can lead to a comprehensive blog post, which in turn drives email sign-ups.

Integrating all marketing channels into a harmonious strategy is like conducting a symphony orchestra. Each element must be attuned to the others, playing its part in creating a unified and compelling narrative. This segment is not just a guide but a call to action for marketers to think holistically, act strategically, and ensure that every channel works in concert towards common goals. By mastering the art of multichannel integration, you can ensure that your marketing efforts resonate with your audience, echoing far beyond the sum of its parts. Remember, in the dynamic world of marketing, harmony isn't just desirable – it's essential.

Revamping Your Game Plan: The Art of Adaptable Marketing

In the ever-shifting landscape of marketing, remaining static is akin to moving backward. This chapter segment focuses on the vital practice of regularly reviewing, revising, and rejuvenating your marketing strategy to stay relevant and effective.

Regularly Reviewing Marketing Performance

Constant assessment is key to maintaining a successful marketing strategy.

- **Set Review Intervals**: Establish regular intervals – monthly, quarterly, or biannually – to evaluate your marketing performance. This keeps you in tune with your strategy's impact.
- **Data-Driven Decisions**: Utilize analytics and performance metrics to make informed decisions. Numbers don't lie; they provide invaluable insights into what works and what doesn't.
- **Comparative Analysis**: Compare current performance against past results and industry benchmarks. This helps in identifying trends and areas needing improvement.

Staying Adaptable to Changing Circumstances

Adaptability is not just a skill; it's a necessity in the dynamic world of marketing.

- **Market Pulse**: Keep your finger on the pulse of market trends and consumer behavior. This awareness enables you to pivot your strategies swiftly as circumstances change.
- **Flexible Frameworks**: Develop marketing strategies with room for flexibility. This way, you can quickly adjust tactics without overhauling your entire plan.
- **Crisis Management**: Have contingency plans in place. This preparation helps you to respond effectively to unforeseen events or crises that could impact your marketing strategy.

Seeking Feedback and Ideas for Improvement

Feedback is the compass that guides your marketing ship in the right direction.

- **Customer Surveys**: Regularly conduct surveys to gather customer feedback. This feedback is a goldmine of insights for improving your marketing strategies.
- **Team Brainstorming**: Involve your team in brainstorming sessions. Different perspectives can lead to innovative ideas and solutions.
- **Open to Criticism**: Embrace constructive criticism and use it as a catalyst for

improvement. It's a powerful tool for refining your marketing approach.

Revisiting and revising your marketing plan is not just a task; it's an ongoing journey of discovery and growth. Embrace the fluidity of the marketing world by staying informed, adaptable, and responsive to feedback. Remember, the only constant in marketing is change. By adopting a mindset of continuous learning and improvement, you position yourself not just to react to changes but to anticipate and leverage them. End each review session not with a period but with a comma, signifying that your marketing story is always evolving, always progressing. Let this segment be your guide in crafting a marketing strategy that is as dynamic and resilient as the market itself.

conclusion

• • •

AS WE REACH the end of this guide, it's essential to remember that marketing a trivia night is more than just a series of strategies and techniques. It's an art form, a blend of creativity, understanding, and a touch of magic. Each page of "How to Market Trivia Night: Skyrocket Your Bar's Popularity with Successful Trivia Marketing" has been a step towards transforming your trivia night into a thriving hub of excitement and community spirit.

The journey through these pages is not just about learning the ins and outs of marketing; it's about embracing a new perspective on how to connect with your audience. It's about seeing your bar not just as a business, but as a gathering place, a stage for unforgettable experiences, and a beacon in your community.

Remember, the heart of a successful trivia night lies in its ability to bring people together, to spark joy, and to create moments that linger in memories. Your role as a marketer is to be the storyteller, the architect of these moments. Every tweet, every email, every poster, and every partnership you forge is a thread in the story you are telling.

As you move forward, keep your ears to the ground and your heart open to feedback. The world of marketing is ever-evolving, and so should your strategies. Stay adaptable, stay curious, and never lose sight of the joy that brought you here in the first place.

Above all, remember that the success of your trivia night is measured not just in numbers, but in the smiles, the laughter, and the community you build. These pages are your guide, but the story is yours to write. Each trivia night is a new chapter, a new opportunity to delight, to engage, and to grow.

So here we are, at the conclusion of this guide, but at the beginning of your adventure. Take these insights, these strategies, and these stories, and weave them into your unique narrative. Your bar, your trivia night, and your community are one-of-a-kind. Celebrate that uniqueness, nurture it, and watch as your trivia night becomes not just an event, but a legend in its own right.

Thank you for joining me on this journey. May your trivia nights be full, your questions challenging, and your community ever-growing. Here's to your success, to nights filled with laughter, and to a future that's brighter than ever. Cheers!

Jon Nelsen

If you need help hosting trivia please check out the companion book:

How to Host Trivia Night: Boost Your Bar's Revenue with Engaging and Memorable Trivia Events - Easy Step-by-Step Guide for Restaurants, Pubs, and Clubs

free resources

. . .

This section contains all the various resources that you will need to get started. If you want to grab these as downloadable PDF's you can head to CheapTrivia.com and we will send them right to your email. →

TEAM SIGNUP

TEAM NAME	# OF PEOPLE	EMAIL

NOTES:

SCORECARD

TEAM NAME	ROUND 1	ROUND 2	ROUND 3	ROUND 4	TOTAL

NOTES:

TRIVIA NIGHT
CHECKLIST

- [ ] **PENS**
- [ ] **ANSWER SHEETS**
- [ ] BUZZERS/BELLS (OPTIONAL)
- [ ] SCORECARD FOR HOST (OPTIONAL)
- [ ] **MICROPHONE AND SOUND SYSTEM (RECOMMENDED)**
- [ ] AUDIOVISUAL EQUIPMENT FOR POWERPOINT (OPTIONAL)
- [ ] **PRIZES FOR 1ST & 2ND PLACE (3RD PLACE IS OPTIONAL)**
- [ ] **PROMOTIONAL MATERIAL (RECOMMENDED)**
- [ ] **TEAM SIGNUP (RECOMMENDED TO COLLECT EMAILS)**
- [ ] **EXTRA BATTERIES**
- [ ] **EXTRA PENS**
- [ ] **SPARE UNTITLED ANSWER SHEETS**

Team Name

#1:

Q	ANSWER	
1		
2		
3		
4		
5		
6		
7		
8		
9		
10		
	ROUND 1 TOTAL	

#2:

Q	ANSWER	
1		
2		
3		
4		
5		
6		
7		
8		
9		
10		
	ROUND 2 TOTAL	

#3:

Q	ANSWER	
1		
2		
3		
4		
5		
6		
7		
8		
9		
10		
	ROUND 3 TOTAL	

#4:

Q	ANSWER	
1		
2		
3		
4		
5		
6		
7		
8		
9		
10		
	ROUND 4 TOTAL	

Job Title: Trivia Night Host
Company: [INSERT RESTAURANT NAME]
Location: [INSERT LOCATION]
Job Type: Part-time

Are you the life of the party, quick with a joke, and have a penchant for facts? [INSERT RESTAURANT NAME] is seeking an enthusiastic and charismatic Trivia Night Host to elevate our weekly trivia events. Join us to transform an ordinary evening into an extraordinary gathering of fun, laughter, and friendly competition. This is the perfect role for someone who thrives in a social atmosphere and loves to entertain a crowd.

Responsibilities:

- Prepare and host trivia nights, ensuring each event runs smoothly from start to finish.
- Engage with participants to create a lively, interactive, and enjoyable environment.
- Craft and deliver trivia questions across various categories, ensuring a balance between challenge and fun.
- Manage the setup and operation of audiovisual equipment to display trivia questions and keep score.
- Promote the event through engaging announcements and interactions to boost attendance and excitement.
- Handle unexpected situations with grace and maintain a positive atmosphere.
- Collect, grade, and announce trivia answers and scores.
- Coordinate with venue staff to optimize seating arrangements and ensure all necessary supplies are available.
- Follow up on event success and gather feedback to improve future trivia nights.

Qualifications:

1. Strong public speaking skills and ability to command an audience.
2. Excellent interpersonal skills; must be outgoing and able to connect with a diverse group of people.
3. Experience in hosting events, quizzes, or performances is highly preferred.
4. Ability to handle AV equipment and troubleshoot basic technical issues.
5. Flexible schedule, primarily evenings, and must be available to host on designated trivia nights.
6. A great sense of humor and a quick wit.
7. Passionate about creating fun and engaging community events.

Benefits:

- Competitive pay rate plus potential tips.
- Flexible part-time hours.
- Opportunity to work in a dynamic and fun environment.
- Discounts on food and beverages at [INSERT RESTAURANT NAME].

How to Apply:

If you're ready to bring your vibrant energy and trivia expertise to [INSERT RESTAURANT NAME], please send your resume and a brief cover letter explaining why you would be the perfect Trivia Night Host to [INSERT EMAIL OR APPLICATION LINK]. We can't wait to meet the next star of our weekly trivia night!

Feel free to adapt the company name, location, and application instructions to fit the specific needs and details of your restaurant. This job description aims to attract candidates who are not only knowledgeable but also have the charisma and energy to make trivia night a standout event.

need marketing
materials & support?
. . .

Everything You Need to Start Booming Trivia Night Try
Us FREE for Two Weeks!

Check out what we offer on the next pages!

Weekly
TRIVIA SUBSCRIPTION
Email Service

QUESTIONS | ANSWERS | HANDOUTS

52 Customizable
TWITTER POST
Canva Templates

TWEET YOUR TRIVIA NIGHTS RIGHT!

52 Customizable

FACEBOOK POST

Canva Templates

SHARE YOUR TRIVIA NIGHTS!

52 Customizable

INSTAGRAM POST

Canva Templates

SHOW OFF YOUR TRIVIA EVENT!

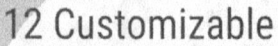

12 Customizable
POSTER TEMPLATES
Canva Ready

PROMOTE YOUR TRIVIA NIGHTS!

Social Media
TEXT & HASHTAG
Templates

SAY THE RIGHT
THINGS TO THE
RIGHT AUDIENCE

52 High-Converting
EMAIL TEMPLATES

EMAILS THAT DELIVER!

How to Host
TRIVIA NIGHT

BOOST YOUR BAR'S REVENUE
WITH ENGAGING & MEMORABLE
TRIVIA EVENTS

How to Market

TRIVIA NIGHT

SKYROCKET YOUR BAR'S
POPULARITY WITH SUCCESSFUL
TRIVIA MARKETING

Ultimate Trivia

MARKETING BUNDLE

All-In-One Social
Media & Trivia
Package!